THE PRESENT TASK
IN NEW TESTAMENT
STUDIES

THE PRESENT TASK IN NEW TESTAMENT STUDIES

AN INAUGURAL LECTURE
DELIVERED IN THE DIVINITY SCHOOL
ON TUESDAY 2 JUNE 1936

BY

C. H. DODD

*Norris–Hulse Professor of Divinity
in the University of Cambridge*

CAMBRIDGE
AT THE UNIVERSITY PRESS
1936

CAMBRIDGE
UNIVERSITY PRESS

University Printing House, Cambridge CB2 8BS, United Kingdom

Published in the United States of America by Cambridge University Press, New York

Cambridge University Press is part of the University of Cambridge.

It furthers the University's mission by disseminating knowledge in the pursuit of
education, learning and research at the highest international levels of excellence.

www.cambridge.org
Information on this title: www.cambridge.org/9781107635456

© Cambridge University Press 1936

First published 1936
Re-issued 2014

A catalogue record for this publication is available from the British Library

ISBN 978-1-107-63545-6 Paperback

THE
PRESENT TASK
IN NEW TESTAMENT
STUDIES

It is impossible for me to stand before you on this occasion without thinking, as you all think, of the great scholar whose death was so severe a loss to our studies, and whose place I unworthily occupy. Francis Crawford Burkitt stood in the high succession of Cambridge theological scholarship. Of his personal qualities it is not fitting that I, a stranger here, whose opportunities of converse with him upon our common interests were too rare, though greatly valued, should speak to you who knew him. He was not only a master in biblical criticism and interpretation, but he had command of vast and recondite learning in the strange regions that lie between Greek-speaking Christendom and the East; and he had that without which learning goes lame, the wisdom to discern significance, which gave authority to his judgment upon tangled problems where so many of the learned fall into extravagance. When some new and startling theory burst upon us, did we not wait and ask, "What will Burkitt say?" His weight of learning was worn lightly, and with an almost boyish freshness of mind, which he kept to the end. He was prodigal in sharing the resources of his knowledge and wisdom with others, and particularly with us younger men, who were stimulated by his unfailing zest for his subject, instructed by his mastery of method, and kept up to scratch by the example of his thoroughness, accuracy and honesty of mind. Much learning has died with him, but his achievement remains both as a sure foundation for further studies, and as an inspiration to those who labour at the same unending task.

It is my intention on this occasion to speak about the nature of that task, in the special field of New Testament studies, as it presents itself to us in this year of grace.

The study of the New Testament falls

naturally into various departments, which may be ideally arranged as stages in a structure. The foundations are laid in textual criticism, the aim of which, never fully attainable, is to restore the text of the several documents as they left the hands of their authors. The text secure, those questions may be raised which belong to what is called the higher criticism. At this stage we seek to determine the date and authorship of the several documents, the circumstances in which they were produced, their sources, the method of their composition, and, so far as they have an historical character, their trustworthiness. The next stage is detailed and exact exegesis of the text. This demands the support of studies which belong to a wider field: the study of the Greek language in its classical, Hellenistic, Byzantine and modern forms, and of the Semitic languages, Hebrew, Aramaic and Syriac. These studies may be pictured as external buttresses to the structure. Upon exact exegesis in turn rests interpretation in the larger sense. At this stage once again the structure needs external buttresses. The thought of the

New Testament cannot be clearly understood without a study of other forms of religious thought and belief with which it stood in historical relations: the Old Testament, Judaism, Greek philosophy, Hellenistic religion with its admixture of oriental elements, and finally the developing thought of the Christian Church after the New Testament period. It is in the light of such studies that we may hope to approximate by degrees to a clear and conclusive understanding of the essential purport of the New Testament in its various parts and as a whole, which is the goal of interpretation. Interpretation in this sense culminates in biblical theology, which is the ἀκρογωνιαῖον of the whole building.

The structural view of New Testament studies which I have thus sketched is an ideal scheme, never fully realized. At each stage we must be content with something less than finality before approaching the next stage. We cannot wait until the archetypal text has been restored before beginning higher criticism or exegesis; and although interpretation must rest upon detailed exegesis, yet the precise sense of a particular passage must often remain undetermined until the meaning of the work as a whole is in some measure understood. All the several departments are to a greater or less extent interdependent. In actual practice the study of the New Testament has advanced by correlated efforts to solve the problems from various points of approach, and further advance must certainly be sought by co-operation of specialists in many fields.

Nevertheless it appears that particular generations of students have found a special attraction in problems of a particular order, and have been specially successful in their solution. It would, I suppose, be generally agreed that textual criticism had a great age in the period which may be roughly defined by the years 1840, which Tischendorf mentions as the beginning of his work, and 1881, which saw the publication of Westcott and Hort's text. During that period the gains of much past work were gathered up, fresh material emerged, principles were laid down, and results were secured which remain valid. It may be that textual criticism will prove to have entered upon another great age, when the remarkable discoveries of the last two or three decades have been fully assimilated. But for the present, though we are being given a "new Tischendorf", it is still based upon the text of Westcott and Hort.

Again, the latter half of the nineteenth century, particularly, perhaps, its last quarter, was a golden age of higher criticism. The Synoptic Problem was, in principle, solved, the Pauline Corpus, within limits, fixed, and the general succession of the New Testament literature determined on lines which all subsequent study assumes as a basis.

The early years of the present century saw a perceptible slowing down of critical advance. This was partly due to the very fact that the major problems had in a measure been solved. In some fields all that remained was to clarify results already attained, to confirm them by more minute tests, and to supplement them by subsidiary hypotheses. Thus, further work on the Synoptic Problem concerned such questions as the relation of Mark and "Q", the unity (or otherwise) of those parts of Matthew and Luke which are not derivable from these primary sources, the process of composition in the First and Third Gospels, and the inner structure of Mark. In Pauline criticism, the non-Pauline character of the Pastoral Epistles (at least in their extant form) has been more definitely established, while the authenticity of Ephesians, and perhaps of II Thessalonians, remains in the balance. For the rest, criticism has tended to concern itself with such subordinate questions as the possibly composite character of certain epistles, and with their precise chronological order. On the Acts of the Apostles we have had during this century work on the grand scale, but in its strictly critical aspect it cannot be said to have advanced greatly beyond what was done thirty years ago, except in the way of confirming and supplementing earlier results. In a word, we have been tidying up the situation left by the great critics of the last century.

There is indeed one major problem which the nineteenth century left unsolved, that of the Fourth Gospel. Upon this problem the present century has seen important though as yet inconclusive work, about which I shall have something to say presently. But with this exception it would be true to say that interest has very largely shifted from criticism to other departments. I shall try to show that this shift has led us to a more direct concern with the task of interpretation. No age indeed has been indifferent to this task; but unless I have mistaken the trend of our time, it has become definitely more urgent for us than it was in the recent past. Much of the most interesting contemporary work belongs to this part of the field. It is, I think, in relation to the Pauline Epistles that the work of interpretation is furthest advanced, perhaps because the major critical problems here were comparatively straightforward, and were early solved. But in other fields too the same tendency may be observed.

If we are to select any particular field in which the early years of the present century were specially distinguished, we should, I think, naturally turn to those studies which I described as external buttresses of the New Testament edifice. In the closing years of the nineteenth century the development of the historical and comparative study of religions had its effect upon our studies. Attention began to be directed towards the background and environment of early Christianity. Our science moved from anatomy to oecology, the study of the organism in its habitat.

There have been here two main lines of approach. On the one hand the study of Judaism in and about the New Testament period began to take on a fresh importance, as the somewhat one-sided emphasis on the apocalyptic literature was corrected, and the results of a more scientific examination of the Rabbinic material became available. Thirty years ago we still depended largely upon John Lightfoot's *Horae Hebraicae et Talmudicae*, published in 1674, and upon the now discredited Weber. To-day a whole series of works, from the Jewish as well as from the Christian side, are at our disposal.

On the other hand, the so-called *Religions-*

geschichtliche Schule set out to exploit for New Testament purposes a mass of material gathered from the wide and varied world of Hellenistic religion, with its extensive background in the older religions not only of Greece but of the whole Near East. It is perhaps in this direction that the most distinctive contribution of the first quarter of the twentieth century will be found to lie. The value of such material depends on the use made of it. Our commentaries have indeed been enriched with an astonishing assortment of "parallels" diligently collected from every part of the Hellenistic underworld. The observation, however, of so many isolated parallels may be confusing rather than enlightening. They are often adduced as evidence for the "derivation" of this or that element in early Christianity from Hellenistic sources of one kind or another. But here we should do well to be cautious. Something more than a simple parallel is needed to prove derivation. It may be suspected that some of those who apply this method of research are still working with categories left over by the higher critics.

Higher criticism necessarily and rightly enquires after sources and derivations, and employs comparative methods to determine them. But this lies within a sphere in which the documents are related to one another by the very conditions of their production. But to establish derivations outside this sphere is a more speculative enterprise; and it is in any case not of the first importance, since to establish the derivation of an idea is not to explain it as an element in a new complex.

The full value of such comparative studies is revealed only when a serious attempt is made to envisage the religious environment as a whole, with its various components accurately differentiated and related one to another, and then to envisage the Christian religion as a whole within that environment. My impression, however, is that many such attempts so far have something hasty and premature about them. Their implied estimate of early Christianity as one more amalgam of half-digested ideas drawn from Hellenistic sources, with a larger contribution from popular Judaism than is usual in such amalgams, is made possible only by an insufficiently critical treatment of the external material, and by an inadequate comprehension of the specific character of the New Testament itself. In a word, the work of the school to which I have referred is a direct challenge to the student of the New Testament to conceive the Canon as the expression of a distinctive movement of life and thought, to be described, and not only described but interpreted, in the light of an environment which we are coming to know better than it has ever been known before. That is to say, it brings the problems of interpretation, rather than of criticism, well into the foreground.

To the study of the Hellenistic environment belongs also the investigation of the Greek language in the New Testament period. The intensive study of Greek papyri and inscriptions for this purpose belongs pre-eminently to the period about the turn of the centuries, and its enlargement of our accurate knowledge of Hellenistic Greek, in those forms of it which are nearest to the language of the New Testament, is one of the great achievements of the time. In the first enthusiasm of the new linguistic discoveries there was perhaps a tendency in some quarters to assume that for the exegesis of the New Testament nothing more was needed than to ascertain the meaning and usage of words among the traders and farmers of Hellenistic Egypt, who are the principal authors of the non-literary papyri. But this is clearly not enough. In these last years the study of New Testament Greek seems to have entered upon a fresh phase, of which the great *Theologisches Wörterbuch zum Neuen Testament*, now in process of publication, is typical. While exploiting the results of the study of papyri and inscriptions, it recognizes that such "external lexicography" (as the editor of the *Wörterbuch* calls it) is only the first stage. In order really to understand the terms employed by the writers of the New Testament, we must consider them as they appear within that specific movement of the spirit of man which is early Christianity. This movement is to be seen taking up the current language of the time, and constraining it masterfully to express its own creative ideas. The illumination which results from this manner of approach (in spite of occasional extravagances) is a matter of experience for all who have used the parts already issued of this remarkable work. The outcome of it is that in attempting the exegesis of any particular passage, we are referred back to the whole context of early Christian life and thought, within which the terms used acquire their specific significance. While approaching exegesis from the exact study of words, we find ourselves fairly embarked upon the task of interpretation in the larger sense.

In this task we are greatly assisted by linguistic research in the adjoining field of Semitics. While knowledge of the Aramaic language as spoken by Jesus Christ and His apostles is still very imperfect, learned Semitists are laying us under a great obligation by their elucidation of its idiom as it underlies the Greek text of the Gospels and other New Testament documents. At least we are aware that neither the critic nor the exegete may safely neglect the Semitic factor, and that interpretation must always take account of an idiom, not only of language but of thought, which is not purely Greek.

In the years following the war there has been in one direction a return to criticism. Fresh interest in the Synoptic Problem has been aroused by the emergence of a new method, known, not too felicitously, as *Formgeschichte*, or "Form-criticism". Its advocates recognize that the familiar methods of documentary criticism succeeded in determining the literary relations of the Synoptic Gospels, but that their success has been strictly limited in dealing with the pre-literary phase of the tradition. This phase, however, is of great importance, since it was in the period between the death of Christ and the beginnings of Gospel writing that the tradition was formed. Let us then, they say, examine the forms in which the tradition may be assumed to have reached the compilers of our Gospels, or their immediate sources, with a view to discovering its character in the oral stage. With this aim, they undertake to identify the characteristic patterns into which various elements in the Gospel tradition fall—aphorisms, parables, ethical precepts, narratives introducing significant pronouncements, biographical narratives, miracle-stories, and so forth. These patterns are conceived as being constituted in accordance with fixed laws of folk-tradition, observable also in other fields than that of Christian antiquity. For purposes of critical study their distinctive content may be neglected, and the patterns classified under headings which would equally well fit pagan or Jewish traditions of a similar character.

A botanical classification, however, though it has its uses, is not an inspiring affair. If that were all, it would be difficult to account for the enthusiasm with which the new method has been received among younger students, at least in Germany, or for the undoubted fact that it has brought new life into the criticism of the Gospels. The form-critics do themselves injustice in suggesting that they aim merely at an arid classification of formal patterns to the neglect of the content. The real interest of the method lies in the attempt to relate the several "forms" to various aspects of the life of the Church which employed them to convey its tradition. The quest for the "setting in life" (*Sitz im Leben*) compels the student to keep steadily in mind something which lies beyond the merely formal analysis of the Gospel material, namely the history of the primitive Christian community as a living and growing thing, expressing itself through various forms of tradition. That is why I consider the term "Form-criticism" to be a somewhat misleading title for a method which leads us away from the rigorous externality of literary or source-criticism, and attempts to read the Gospels from within as the product of a living process, which we must understand in order to give an account of their origin and character.

It is significant that the newer critics invite our especial attention to elements in the Gospels which the earlier critics neglected. They were dominated by a too narrow view of history, and in their "quest of the historical Jesus" they put aside with something like contempt anything which might conceivably be attributed to the thought and experience of the early Church, hoping in this way to arrive at a substratum of bare fact. In doing so, they were rejecting elements of prime value for the understanding of the Gospels, much as we are told that in the milling of our flour the vitamins are eliminated and cast away as refuse. The interpretation of the Synoptic Gospels was hampered because a narrowly literary criticism left an inevitable gap between the facts of the life of Jesus and their earliest literary record—a gap offering tempting opportunities for guesswork. In so far as the gap is being closed by scientific study of the pre-literary tradition, the way is being opened for a more adequate interpretation.

We are led in a similar direction if we consider the present position of Johannine criticism. If the solution of the Synoptic Problem was the most spectacular success of the nineteenth-century critics, the Johannine Problem represents their most signal failure. The position at the end of the century was little better than a deadlock.

Conservatives on the one hand and liberals on the other could damage each other's case, but neither could produce convincing arguments for their own. The two views were radically incompatible; both could not be true, and no way of accommodation commended itself. Progress promised to begin when it was admitted on both sides that the document before us was not, in the full sense, the "seamless robe" which both schools had assumed it to be. With that admission began the belated attempt to analyse the Fourth Gospel, like the Synoptics, into *strata* and sources. During the present century hypotheses innumerable have been offered—partition hypotheses, displacement hypotheses, theories of oral and written sources, of editorial redaction, and so forth. It may be that in one of these hypotheses lies the key to the ultimate solution, as the key of the Synoptic Problem lay in Weisse's *Marcushypothese* of 1836, though it was many years before that key was proved to be capable of opening the lock. But so far no particular theory shows signs of general acceptance.

The reason why the higher criticism of the Fourth Gospel lags behind that of the Synoptic Gospels is manifest. It lies in the nature of the documents that the methods applicable to the first three Gospels are not in the same way applicable to the fourth. Synoptic criticism began its successful career when critics renounced all *a priori* assumptions about the character of the several Gospels, and even (for their immediate purpose) all direct interest in their contents, and confined their attention to external, concrete, measurable facts, such as words and their arrangement, grammatical forms, percentages of expressions common to two or more Gospels, relative length of sections, and order of sections. All the data necessary for the fundamental solution of the Synoptic Problem can be exhibited by marking the text of a synopsis, as for instance they are exhibited in Rushbrooke's *Synopticon*. Consideration and comparison of the ideas of the several evangelists may confirm and illustrate their relationships, but the Two-document Theory stands independently of any such consideration. That is why the solution of the Synoptic Problem can be stated with an artistic completeness and elegance which charms the critical mind.

As we have already seen, this method no longer serves when we attempt to analyse our earliest Gospel, or to go behind the written sources of the Gospels to the oral tradition behind them. No more do they avail for the analysis of the Fourth Gospel. The extent to which this Gospel overlaps the others is too slight to give us a sufficient basis for detailed comparison. Within the book itself, the changes of language, if such there be, are not clearly enough marked to serve as a safe clue to source analysis. The evangelist no doubt recurs to certain forms of expression in certain sections, but this may be due (for all we know) to his habit of mind rather than to the use of different sources. At best it may be possible to mark a sentence here and there as suggesting by its terms, or by the grammatical construction of the passage, the work of an editor; but for any far-reaching analysis we do not seem at present to have sufficient evidence in the concrete, external facts of language and form, though it seems possible that the Aramaists may have something to say about this. In any case, the attempt to distinguish various *strata* depends far more on a consideration of the ideas and the intention of the writer, and before it can have any cogency we must be sure that we understand what he is about.

To give an example, theories of diverse sources have been founded upon the fact that the evangelist speaks in various ways of the Son of Man being "lifted up" (ὑψωθῆναι), sometimes in a way which suggests the exaltation of Christ to heavenly glory and dominion, sometimes in a way which suggests a mystical exaltation of the ideal humanity, and sometimes in a way which suggests the "lifting up" of the body of Jesus in crucifixion. But what if it be a mark of this evangelist's thought that he deliberately unites all these ideas under one expression? We cannot know until we have in some measure understood the Gospel as a whole.

Again, for some critics it is plain that the original framework of the Fourth Gospel was an historical and chronological narrative of the ministry of Jesus, and that the theological material interwoven with it represents either a different source or the work of a later commentator. For others it is equally plain that the fundamental *stratum* of the Gospel is a series of theological discourses, and that the apparently historical matter is redactional. The one theory or the other is adopted, nor primarily on the ground of measurable linguistic or other phenomena, but as a result of one view or another of the purport of the work. How do we know that precisely this combination of a certain elaborateness, even pedantry, of narrative detail, with a mystical spirituality, is not the essential stamp of the author's mind? In short, the problem of criticism resolves itself into a problem of interpretation.

The most fruitful work that has been done recently on the Fourth Gospel is probably not along the line of critical analysis. Indeed interest in critical questions of date, authorship and sources appears lately to have subsided. Greater interest has been aroused by the study of the background of Johannine thought, Jewish and Hellenistic. Perhaps in no other part of the New Testament has the work of the *Religionsgeschichtliche Schule* been more richly suggestive. This work will probably prove to have value, when combined with the methods of "Form-criticism", for definitely critical purposes, if it can be shown that certain sections betray a "setting in life" within a Palestinian Jewish environment, while other portions are at home in the Hellenistic world. But its primary value is for interpretation. We really do seem to be approaching the point at which the baffling thought of the Fourth Gospel begins to clarify itself by being intelligibly related to a known environment. It is not that we can classify this element as derived from Rabbinic Judaism, that from Philo, another from the Hermetica, or Gnosticism, or Mandaism. Here, as in other fields, the question of derivation is of secondary importance, even supposing it could be convincingly answered.

It is that when we have acclimatized ourselves in the atmosphere which surrounded the author and his first readers, his distinctive contribution to religious thought leaps to the eye. Profound and original as the teaching of the Fourth Gospel has always been acknowledged to be, its profundity and originality become more impressive than ever when we approach it from this side.

I am disposed to think that the understanding of this Gospel is not only one of the outstanding tasks of our time, but the crucial test of our success or failure in solving the problem of the New Testament as a whole. The Fourth Gospel may well prove to be the keystone of an arch which at present fails to hold together. If we can understand it, understand how it came to be and what it means, we shall know what early Christianity really was, and not until in some measure we comprehend the New Testament as a whole shall we be in a position to solve the Johannine Problem.

All these observations tend, as it seems to me, to the conclusion that students of the New

Testament at this particular time are being driven by the logic of the situation to a direct attack on the problem of interpretation. That interpretation is the goal of our studies would no doubt have been recognized in all periods, and it has never been entirely neglected. But there have been times when students have felt obliged to deny themselves the satisfaction of handling it until prior problems should have been elucidated. We are no longer in this position. Thanks to the labours of our predecessors we have enough accurate knowledge available, in the fields of textual criticism, higher criticism, background and language, to provide a starting-point. There are, it is true, many unsolved problems in criticism; the investigation of the background is in many respects incomplete; questions of uncertain exegesis are always with us, and always will be. There is room enough for the work of specialists in every field. But the point, I believe, has been reached, at which further progress, even in special fields, depends upon our treating them in direct relation to the over-ruling problem of interpretation. Already much of the best work of our time is moving, consciously or unconsciously, in this direction. The present task, as I believe, is to make interpretation the conscious and direct aim of our studies in whatever special field they may lie. Of the risks involved I am not unaware. Premature schemes of interpretation in the past are our warning. But we must take the risks, or condemn our studies to sterility.

The kind of interpretation I have in mind will in one sense reverse the main direction in which New Testament studies moved for a century. Our principal aim has hitherto been to discriminate as clearly as possible between various books and *strata*, so as to isolate for intensive study the special problems connected with each separate part; for example the Pauline Epistles, the Fourth Gospel, the Synoptic Gospels, and within these the Marcan *stratum*, the "Q" *stratum*, and so forth. This process of analysis should now be balanced by a movement in the opposite direction. I will not call it synthesis, for that term might imply the imposition of unity upon originally disparate material. But the unity of the New Testament is original, underlying the diversity of the individual writings. These writings have come down to us in the form of a Canon, representing the judgment of the early Church—of those best qualified to judge—that in them the Christian religion as a whole received authoritative expression, under a diversity of manifestations, but by the same Spirit. This fact is of primary significance for the interpreter of the Canon.

The influence of analytical criticism upon the interpretation of the New Testament was far-reaching, and not in all respects beneficial. Unquestionably the method of isolating certain ideas as characteristic of this or that portion of the New Testament, which could be assigned to a particular date and historical situation, was in its time of quite incalculable value for clear thinking, and opened a fruitful period of investigation. But its exclusive dominance led to a piecemeal treatment of early Christian thought, which in the end made it more difficult to understand the New Testament as a whole, and left the mind bewildered by its diversity. This could be observed even in works which set out to expound comprehensively the Theology of the New Testament. Such works were often found to be rather of the nature of encyclopaedias of early Christian doctrines, each treated in a separate article. It was this kind of treatment that led to the propounding of unreal dilemmas, such as "Jesus or Paul?" "The Jesus of history or the Christ of the Fourth Gospel?" "Eschatology or Ethics?" These dilemmas arise only when the departmental treatment of the New Testament is pushed to an exclusive extreme.

The case becomes even more serious when the method of the comparative study of religions is applied to the New Testament thus dissected, without regard to its inner unity. For example: in the Synoptic Gospels we meet with the idea of the "Kingdom of God"; an idea characteristic of Paul is expressed in his formula "in Christ"; and in the Fourth Gospel the idea of the Logos plays an important part.

Now isolate each of these, and examine them in their relations with the environment in each case. The examination of the idea of the Kingdom of God leads us not only to Hebrew ideas of theocracy in the Old Testament and to Jewish apocalyptic writings, but also, it is suggested, to Zoroastrianism, and even to primitive Aryan conceptions. The Pauline "Christ-mysticism" suggests analogies in Hellenistic and oriental mysticism. The Logos idea has links both with Jewish theosophy and with Stoicism and Platonism, and a background, as some would have it, in Egyptian and Iranian mythology. Thus each idea is illustrated by a method which leads us farther and farther from any common centre to which they may have been related in early Christianity. But meanwhile it is certain that the early Church, which incorporated the several documents in the Canon, believed that the inmost secret of its life was variously expressed in the propositions, "The Kingdom of God is at hand"—"If any man is in Christ there is a new creation"— "The Logos was made flesh and dwelt among us." The centrifugal movement needs to be balanced by a centripetal movement which will bring these ideas, now better understood in their individual character, into the unity of the life that originally informed them. The emphasis laid in some recent work upon this principle of inner unity, as controlling all specialized research in the New Testament field, is a sign that we have entered upon a new stage of interpretation.

For Christianity, however it arose, is a distinct phenomenon in the spiritual life of mankind. It is not to be confused with anything else, however close its resemblance may be, in certain respects, to other spiritual movements, and however real its affinities with them. Nor is it a mere collocation of various religious ideas, but an organic unity. It is the task of New Testament study to understand this phenomenon for what it is in itself, in its characteristic unity as well as in its diversity.

This task would not be fully achieved if we should succeed in constructing a scheme of the genetic development of early Christianity. We have not yet succeeded in doing so. Neither the scheme of the early Tübingen School, which was based upon the Hegelian dialectic, nor the scheme offered by nineteenth-century liberalism, which bears the stamp of biological theories of evolution, fits the known facts satisfactorily. Indeed, the application of the category of development is peculiarly difficult in a case where our series of documents covers only a century, while the really significant development must on any showing have taken place in the twenty years or so before the earliest of these documents were written. Nor is the development within the New Testament like that of a school of philosophy or learning. The writers do not succeed one another, as in the Stoic School Zeno was succeeded by Cleanthes, and Cleanthes by Chrysippus, though some criticism seems unconsciously to assume that they did.

It lies before us as the deposit of a spiritual movement, whose historical form was a religious society of persons of various race, antecedents, education and outlook, but intensely

conscious of their unity in the Spirit. The life of
the society embodied itself in institutions, in
discipline, in cultus and sacrament, and in
preaching and teaching. Its beliefs and con-
victions were expressed in many varied forms—
in stories about the Lord and His earliest fol-
lowers, in aphorisms and discourses representing the tradition of His teaching, in letters,
epistles, sermons and theological and ethical
tractates, in hymns and liturgies. It is out of
such materials that the New Testament is com-
posed. But through it all one dominant theme
can be heard, that theme which the early
Church called εὐαγγέλιον, "the Gospel". To
interpret the New Testament is to understand
the various forms which the Gospel takes in
such a way as to understand the Gospel itself.

Our study is in the first place historical, for it
aims at the interpretation of that significant
phenomenon in history which is early Christianity. Such study is peculiarly relevant to a
religion which so emphatically announces itself
as an historical revelation. But the interpreter I
have in mind will be one who, having pene-

trated to the historical actuality of first-century Christianity, has received an impression of the truth in it which lies beyond the flux of time, and demands to be re-stated in terms intelligible to the mind of our own age. It is not that the thought of the twentieth century is, as such, superior in validity to that of the first century, but that no truth can be communicated, or even fully grasped, until it can be naturalized, in any age whatever.

The problem of interpretation has not been fully comprehended, to my mind, if it be conceived as an attempt to disengage (according to a popular formula) the "permanent" element in the New Testament from its "temporary" setting. Whatever is true is permanently true; but there is no such thing, for us, as disembodied truth, nor an expression of truth which is timeless—unless mathematical formulae be considered such an expression. Nor again does an idea necessarily remain true if it is disengaged from a context with which it forms a living whole. There is one sense in which the whole of the New Testament is temporary; for it represents a coherent body of belief related all through to a definite period of thought. Not to have realized this is to have failed to be thorough in criticism and exegesis. In another sense none of it is merely temporary, if it be true at all. No attempt to extract particular elements from it, and to exhibit these as "permanent" in isolation from the rest, can be other than superficial.

I may perhaps make my meaning clearer by an example. It has been felt that the eschatological element in the New Testament might safely be written off as "temporary". Certainly it is alien from our modern ways of thought. But closely related to it is the idea of the Kingdom of God, which lies at the heart of the Gospels. This idea, it was supposed, could be separated from the eschatological context in which it has come down to us, and understood in a sense congenial to the humanitarian idealism of the pre-war period, as a Utopian ideal of social progress. The result was to draw a veil between our minds and a great part of the Gospels. Not only so, but the idea of the Kingdom of God, so understood, seemed to have no relation to other New Testament conceptions, such as those of redemption and eternal life. These too come down to us in an eschatological setting; but eschatology having been relegated to a museum of antiquities, the ideas hung in the air. But in the New Testament the ideas of redemption, eternal life, and the Kingdom of God emerge in a total context which includes at every point those eschatological ideas which were rejected as temporary. In this sense the idea of the Kingdom of God is also temporary. Our task is not thus to pick and choose, but to grasp the whole first-century Gospel in its temporary, historical, and therefore actual, reality, and then to make the bold and even perilous attempt to translate the whole into contemporary terms.

The ideal interpreter would be one who has entered into that strange first-century world, has felt its whole strangeness, has sojourned in it until he has lived himself into it, thinking and feeling as one of those to whom the Gospel first came; and who will then return into our world, and give to the truth he has discerned a body out of the stuff of our own thought. If there are other qualifications of which it is less fitting to speak in an academic lecture, I may be allowed to hint at them in a phrase familiar to theologians—*testimonium Spiritus Sancti internum*.

This is an ideal. That any of us, or all of us together, will be able to realize it fully, or to give a final interpretation of the New Testament, final even for our own age, is not to be supposed. But here our task lies.